Praying Mantis

Elizabeth J. Scholl

KIDHAVEN
PRESS™

THOMSON
GALE

San Diego • Detroit • New York • San Francisco • Cleveland
New Haven, Conn. • Waterville, Maine • London • Munich

LIBRARY OF CONGRESS CATALOGING-IN-PUBLICATION DATA

Scholl, Elizabeth J.
  Praying Mantis / by Elizabeth Scholl.
    p. cm.—(Bugs)
Summary: Describes the physical characteristics, behavior, and habitat of the praying mantis.
Includes bibliographical references.
  ISBN 0-7377-1773-4 (hardcover : alk. paper)
1. Praying mantis—Juvenile literature. [1. Praying mantis.] I. Title. II. Series.
  QL505.9.M35S36 2004
  595.7'27—dc22

2003012843

Printed in China

CONTENTS

Same and Different

There are about eighteen hundred types of praying mantises. Mantises are found in temperate, tropical, and subtropical regions. They live on every continent except Antarctica. Although they all share certain features, mantises vary by color.

Most praying mantises are brown or green, but some are white, pink, or purple. The purple-winged mantis has a brown body and green eyes, with purple

Opposite: A praying mantis's head is shown magnified many times its normal size.

5

The Malaysian orchid mantis resembles the petals of an orchid flower.

wings. European mantises can change color from brown to green, depending on whether their environment is wet and green or dry and brown.

Sizes and Shapes

Praying mantises also vary greatly in size. Most grow to between two and five inches in length, but some are smaller and some much larger. The *Bolbe pygmaea* is one of the smallest mantises. It is less than one inch long. The giant Malaysian mantis can grow to ten inches. Neotropical praying mantises of Central and South America grow so large they can eat hummingbirds and tree frogs!

Some mantises have unusual features. Certain varieties look like tropical flowers. One of the most exotic looking is the Malaysian orchid mantis. It has pink, white, green, and brown markings; pointed eyes; and petal-like shapes on its legs, resembling those of orchid flowers.

Even experts sometimes mistake these mantises for part of the flower.

Asia and Africa host many extraordinary mantises. The wandering violin mantis, also called the giraffe neck mantis, has a very long neck, like that of a violin. It has small, leaflike growths on its head and legs. Its arms look as if they have boxing gloves on the ends. The Madagascan marbled mantis has pink or purple eyes and a marbled pattern all over its body. On its front legs it has black spots that look like large eyes.

The Praying Mantis's Body

Praying mantises share the same three body parts as all insects—the head, the thorax, and the abdomen. They have six legs and two antennae. They have an exoskeleton, or protective skeleton on the outside of their bodies.

Praying mantises have a triangle-shaped head that can turn 180 degrees, in a half circle. Mantises are the only creatures in the insect world that can do this. Their ability to turn

Unlike other insects, the praying mantis can rotate its head a full 180 degrees.

Body of a Praying Mantis

1 Triangle-shaped head can turn from side to side, giving the mantis the ability to see in all directions. Compound eyes have hundreds of lenses and can see prey up to sixty feet away.

2 Hard outer shell, or exoskeleton, protects the mantis's soft body parts. Unique coloring, or camouflage, helps the insect hide from predators and prey.

3 Long, spiked legs and powerful jaws allow the mantis to catch and eat prey much bigger than itself.

their heads from one side to the other helps them to see prey as far away as sixty feet.

Amazing Eyes

The compound eye on each side of the mantis's head gives it excellent eyesight. Like those of other insects, the mantis's compound eyes are made up of hundreds of lenses. Each lens is like an eye itself. What a praying mantis sees with its compound eyes is similar to someone watching hundreds of televisions at once, all tuned to the same channel. In addition to its compound eyes, the mantis has three simple eyes, arranged in a triangle between its antennae. **Entomologists** are scientists who study insects. They believe simple eyes tell the difference between light and dark, while compound eyes see images and colors.

Praying mantises' unique body features combined with the ability to **camouflage** themselves, have helped them adapt to and survive in many types of habitats around the world.

From Egg to Adult

Praying mantises generally live for three to nine months. They hatch from egg sacs in the spring and live until the fall. The life cycle of the praying mantis begins when the female mantis **fertilizes** her eggs with the sperm of the male mantis. In order for this to happen, the male and female mantis must mate.

During mating, the male passes his sperm to the female. She stores it for later use. When mating is complete, the male leaps away quickly. He probably does not want to take any chances—female mantises sometimes bite off the heads of the males during mating! Even if she does this, the male is able to complete the mating process—without his head.

During mating the female mantis (left) sometimes bites off the head of the male.

The Ootheca

About nine days after mating, the female mantis makes an ootheca, or egg case. She hangs upside down from a branch of a tree or shrub, and white foam, like whipped cream, squirts out from her abdomen. She lays her eggs in this foam and then fertilizes them by covering them with stored sperm.

White foam containing hundreds of eggs (below) squirts from the female's abdomen. At right, hundreds of mantis nymphs emerge from an ootheca, or egg case.

Soon the foam hardens into a walnut-sized case. It can hold up to three hundred eggs. The female mantis constructs several egg cases. Her work is done once the cases are made. Soon after this she dies.

The ootheca is remarkably strong. It can survive wind, snow, and rain. In the spring, baby mantises hatch from the egg case.

Nymphs

Baby mantises are called nymphs. When they come out of the ootheca, nymphs are the size of mosquitoes. They look like tiny adult mantises but are the color of honey. As soon as the nymphs emerge, they lower themselves to the ground on a thin thread that drops off as soon as they are able to move around.

Within a few hours, the nymphs shed their skin, allowing them to grow. This is called molting. The nymph molts by hanging upside down from a plant stem. Its skin splits open, and the nymph wriggles out of it. Molting is dangerous because while they are hanging, nymphs can become prey to birds or other insects. Their honey coloring stands out on green leaves, as well as on dark branches or bark. As they cannot hide well, many nymphs are eaten by **predators**.

After the nymph finishes molting, its new skin hardens into an exoskeleton. The nymph will molt six to ten times, becoming larger each time, until it is

A mantis nymph (right) sheds its skin (left) six to ten times before emerging as an adult.

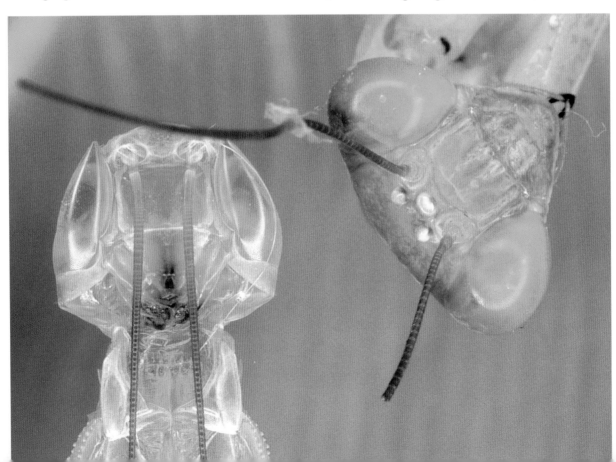

fully grown. The growth stages the mantis goes through are known as **metamorphosis**.

Although hundreds of nymphs come out of an ootheca, only a few survive to adulthood. In addition to the nymphs that fall prey to larger insects, spiders, and birds, many others drown in spring rains.

Young mantises reach adulthood in late summer. Once mantises reach adulthood, they will begin to look for mates to start the life cycle over again.

After reaching adulthood, mantises set out in search of a mate.

From Egg to Adult 15

A Place to Call Home

Praying mantises do not construct homes, such as nests or hives, the way that some insects do. They live on trees, shrubs, flowers, or grass.

Finding the Perfect Home

Mantises find homes where they can hide or camouflage themselves. Many mantises have coloring that mimics, or imitates, the habitats in which they live.

Praying mantises live on trees, shrubs, flowers, or other places where they can camouflage or hide themselves.

Leaf and dead-leaf mantises found in Southeast Asia look like dried, crumpled leaves. That plus their brown, black, or orangey brown coloring helps them blend in with the decaying leaves that are their home. Twig mantises live among the twigs and branches of trees and shrubs in southern Africa. They look just like twigs. They are brownish, and have bumps that resemble those on small branches. Even their eyes look like wood.

At least two types of mantises live on flowers. These mantises look very much like the flowers that are their homes. The Burmese mantis is one. It has a lavender and pink petal-like shape on its thorax, just like

This green leaf mantis hides easily among the leaves of a plant.

the flower that is its home. The pink and green African flower mantis also has petal-like growths on its body. Pink flowers of the rain forest provide a perfect home for this mantis.

Other mantises find homes that also match their looks. The green leaf mantis lives unseen among leaves of plants. A grayish bark mantis mimics its tree trunk home, while a brownish Arizona ground mantis hides easily among shrubs and grasses in dry, sandy areas.

Staying at Home

Adult mantises usually live their whole lives in one place. They tend to stay on one or two bushes or trees throughout their lifetimes. If there is a lot of food available, several mantises may live in one area. If there is not enough food, one mantis may eat the other in order to claim the territory.

Mantises often sit motionless or hang with their heads down and their front legs folded. They are waiting for insects or other small creatures to visit them in their homes. Praying mantises are not very gracious hosts. When other insects land in their homes, they grab and devour them.

In addition to providing a hiding place for mantises, the leaves of the plant on which mantises live provide shelter from the heat of the sun. When it is very hot, mantises go under the leaves to stay cool. They come out to hunt early in the morning and later in the afternoon, when the sun is not so strong.

Whether mantises live on rain-forest flowers or in backyard gardens, they have one thing in common. This is the ability to find homes where they can hide unseen from predators and prey.

Mantises rely on camouflage to remain invisible to both predators and prey.

Grabbing a Bite to Eat

The praying mantis spends most of its time either hunting for food or eating. The mantis is sometimes called the dragon of the insect world because it is such a fierce predator. It attacks just about any insect that crosses its path.

Mantis nymphs are born knowing how to catch food with their long, spiny front legs. As soon as they emerge from their egg case and begin to crawl around, the hunt begins. Nymphs will eat anything they can find that is smaller than they are—tiny flies, aphids, and leafhoppers, to name a few. They will even eat their own brothers and sisters.

Waiting for a Meal

The praying mantis patiently waits for its prey, with its front legs folded in the praying position that gives it its name. Perfectly still, it looks all around for its meal, using its keen eyes and long, flexible neck. The mantis's antennae help it to hear approaching prey. When in reach, the mantis stretches out its spiked legs and, fast as lightning, grabs its prey. Once it is caught, prey rarely escapes the mantis's strong grasp.

The strength of the mantis's spiny forelegs is so great it is able to catch prey larger than itself. Some large mantises can catch lizards, soft-shelled turtles, and small mammals. More commonly, mantises eat insects such as butterflies, moths, wasps, bees, beetles, and katydids.

Praying mantises eat their prey live. First, the mantis bites its head off. This **paralyzes** the prey so

Opposite: A mantis nymph devours a cricket. Mantises spend most of their time hunting for food.

Praying Mantises bite off the heads of their prey before eating the still-living creatures.

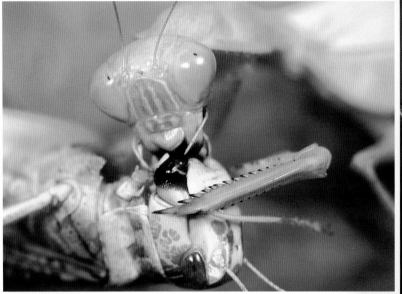

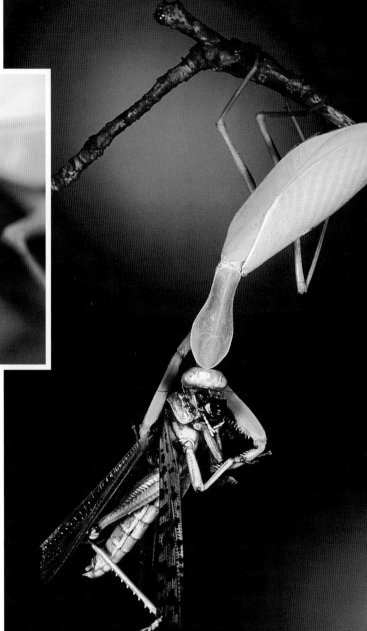

the mantis can finish its meal without a struggle.

After the mantis eats, it cleans itself. It cleans its front legs first, then strokes its head with its front legs, like a cat. Cleaning its eyes and antennae helps the praying mantis to look and listen more clearly for its next meal.

On the Defense

Though adult mantises do not have many enemies in the insect world, they are prey to some birds and bats. Aside from camouflage, some mantises have other unique ways to protect themselves.

Several types of mantises have big spots on their backs. These spots look like large eyes when the mantis spreads its wings. These eye spots surprise the predator, allowing the mantis to make a quick getaway. A few mantises are able to make a hissing noise by rattling their wings, which also can scare predators.

Some mantises have a single ear on the lower part of the thorax. The ear helps praying mantises escape from bats. The mantis's ear hears only **ultrasound**, such as the very high-pitched squeaking of bats. When

Mantises often fall prey to other animals, including other mantises.

A mantis rears up on its hind legs. The praying mantis's speed and hunting skills make the insect a fearsome predator.

the mantis hears a bat, it does what scientists have described as a "power dive." The mantis flies rapidly toward the ground in a spiral motion.

The praying mantis's speed, strength, and patience have made it one of the insect world's most successful predators. These expert hunting skills, combined with its unique adaptations to its habitat, are just a few of the reasons why praying mantises are such fascinating creatures.

GLOSSARY

camouflage: An appearance that hides or disguises animals with colors and patterns that make them look like their surroundings.

entomologist: A scientist who studies insects.

fertilize: To make possible the growth or development of an egg for producing offspring.

metamorphosis: Change in form that some insects go through during their natural development.

paralyze: To make unable to move or do anything.

predator: An animal that catches and eats other animals.

ultrasound: Vibrations that are the same kind as sound waves but have too high a frequency to be heard by the human ear.

FOR FURTHER EXPLORATION

Books

Larry Dane Brimmer, *Praying Mantises.* Danbury, CT: Children Press, 1999. This book describes the characteristics and life cycle of the Chinese mantis, one of the mantises found in the United States.

Bianca Lavies, *Backyard Hunter: The Praying Mantis.* New York: Penguin Books, 1990. This book describes the life cycle of the praying mantis. Great, close-up color photos.

Kathleen Pohl, *The Praying Mantis.* Milwaukee, WI: Raintree, 1987. A short-chapter book that discusses the traits, body parts, and habits of the praying mantis.

Rebecca Stefoff, *Praying Mantis.* Tarrytown, NY: Benchmark Books, 1997. This short, easy-to-read book briefly explains the praying mantis's life cycle and discusses various types of mantises. Nice photographs of some interesting mantises.

Websites

Earth's Birthday Project (www. earths birthday.org). This educational and fun website has information about praying mantises, printable work sheets about mantises, and mantis activities such as "Praying Mantis Geometry."

Insecta Inspecta World (www.insecta-inspecta.com). This website offers a description of praying mantises and information about mantis habitats, diet, and breeding. Information on other insects is also available.

Mantis UK: Home of the Alternative Pet (www.mantisuk.com). This is the website of a company that sells mantises as pets. It has photos and descriptions of many exotic and unusual mantis species from all over the world, along with information about each one.

INDEX

PICTURE CREDITS

ABOUT THE AUTHOR

Elizabeth J. Scholl is a writer of children's books and educational materials. She lives in Hillsdale, New Jersey, with her husband and three children. When not writing, Scholl enjoys watching wildlife, gardening, and bicycling.